A Note to Parents

DK READERS is a compelling program for beginning readers, designed in conjunction with leading literacy experts, including Dr. Linda Gambrell, Professor of Education at Clemson University. Dr. Gambrell has served as President of the National Reading Conference and the College Reading Association, and has recently been elected to serve as President of the International Reading Association.

Beautiful illustrations and superb full-color photographs combine with engaging, easy-to-read stories to offer a fresh approach to each subject in the series. Each DK READER is guaranteed to capture a child's interest while developing his or her reading skills, general knowledge, and love of reading.

The five levels of DK READERS are aimed at different reading abilities, enabling you to choose the books that are exactly right for your child:

Pre-level 1: Learning to read
Level 1: Beginning to read
Level 2: Beginning to read alone
Level 3: Reading alone
Level 4: Proficient readers

The "normal" age at which a child begins to read can be anywhere from three to eight years old. Adult participation through the lower levels is very helpful for providing encouragement, discussing storylines, and sounding out unfamiliar words.

No matter which level you select, you can be sure that you are helping your child learn to read, then read to learn!

DK

LONDON, NEW YORK, MUNICH,
MELBOURNE, and DELHI

For Dorling Kindersley
Editor Hannah Dolan
Designer Rhys Thomas
Design Manager Ron Stobbart
Art Director Lisa Lanzarini
Publishing Manager Catherine Saunders
Publisher Simon Beecroft
Publishing Director Alex Allan
Production Editor Marc Staples
Production Controller Nick Seston
Reading Consultant Dr. Linda Gambrell

For Lucasfilm
Executive Editor J. W. Rinzler
Art Director Troy Alders
Keeper of the Holocron Leland Chee
Director of Publishing Carol Roeder

First published in the United States in 2012
by DK Publishing
345 Hudson Street, New York, New York 10014

10 9 8 7 6 5 4 3 2
006-181961-Oct/11

DK books are available at special discounts when purchased in bulk
for sales promotions, premiums, fund-raising, or educational use.
For details, contact:
DK Publishing Special Markets
345 Hudson Street
New York, New York 10014
SpecialSales@dk.com

A catalog record for this book is available
from the Library of Congress.

ISBN: 978-0-7566-8693-2 (Paperback)
ISBN: 978-0-7566-8692-5 (Hardcover)

Color reproduction by Media Development Printing Ltd., UK
Printed and bound in China by L-Rex

Discover more at
www.dk.com
www.LEGO.com
www.starwars.com

DK READERS

LEGO

STAR WARS

THE PHANTOM MENACE

DK

WRITTEN BY HANNAH DOLAN

The Jedi

Who are these cloaked figures? Meet Qui-Gon Jinn and his apprentice Obi-Wan Kenobi. They are Jedi. The Jedi are peacekeepers of the galaxy. Jedi use a power called the Force to help them protect the galaxy. The Jedi use the Force for good, but it can also be used for evil.

The Force

The Force is an invisible power that flows through everything in the galaxy. The Jedi sometimes use the Force to fight, but only in self-defense.

lightsaber

Jedi hood

Obi-Wan Kenobi   Qui-Gon Jinn

The Trade Federation

Qui-Gon and Obi-Wan travel
across the galaxy on this
Republic Cruiser starship.
Don't tell anyone, but they are
on a secret mission to meet the
Trade Federation.

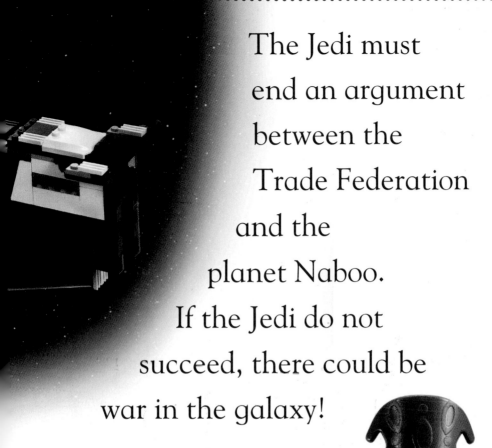

The Jedi must
end an argument
between the
Trade Federation
and the
planet Naboo.
If the Jedi do not
succeed, there could be
war in the galaxy!

This is the person
Qui-Gon and Obi-Wan
have come to see.
He is the greedy leader
of the Trade Federation,
Nute Gunray.

Nute Gunray

Dark dealings

There is something about Nute
Gunray that the Jedi do not know...

He has joined forces with an
evil Sith Lord called Darth Sidious.
Darth Sidious controls Nute
Gunray and the Trade Federation.
He communicates with Nute
Gunray via a hologram.

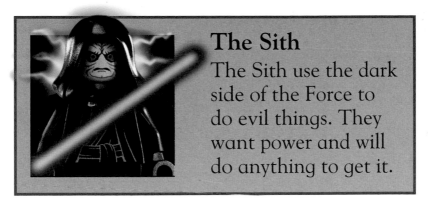

The Sith
The Sith use the dark side of the Force to do evil things. They want power and will do anything to get it.

Darth Sidious tells Nute Gunray to invade Naboo and destroy the Jedi!

escape pod

Invasion of Naboo

The Jedi escape the Trade Federation and land on Naboo. Look out! The Trade Federation's droid army has also arrived!

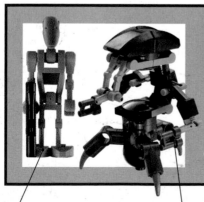

Droid army

Battle droids and droidekas are controlled by a Trade Federation starship above Naboo.

battle droid　　*droideka*

Droids invade Naboo on huge Multi-Troop Transports (MTTs). Hundreds of droids are tightly packed together in the MTTs. They are all programmed to attack the peaceful planet.

Jar Jar Binks

You there, get out of the way!

This is Jar Jar Binks. An MTT almost runs him over, but Qui-Gon saves him just in time! Jar Jar is a Gungan who lives underwater in the Naboo swamps. He helps the Jedi travel to the Queen's Royal Palace in Theed.

The Jedi must find the Queen of Naboo before the droid army does! They race underwater in a Gungan submarine called a bongo.

Queen Amidala
This is the Queen of Naboo, Padmé Amidala. She lives in the Royal Palace. She refuses to give in to the Trade Federation.

Anakin Skywalker

Welcome to Tatooine.
This young slave boy
is Anakin Skywalker.
He belongs to a junk
dealer called Watto.
Anakin works in Watto's junk shop.

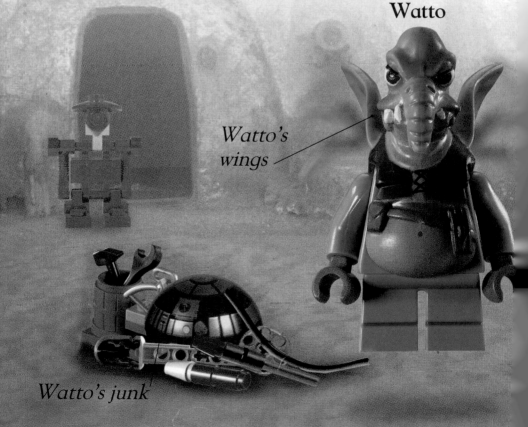

Watto

Watto's
wings

Watto's junk

Qui-Gon Jinn and Queen Amidala arrive at Watto's shop. They escaped Naboo along with Obi-Wan and Jar Jar, but the droid army attacked their ship! They need to find parts to fix it.

Qui-Gon senses that the Force is extremely strong in Anakin. Could he be the "Chosen One"?

The Chosen One
Qui-Gon believes that the Chosen One will one day bring balance to the Force.

Podracing

Anakin is an excellent pilot and he really loves to Podrace.

He even built his own Podracer out of parts from Watto's shop. Just don't tell Watto!

Anakin enters a Podrace called the Boonta Eve Classic.

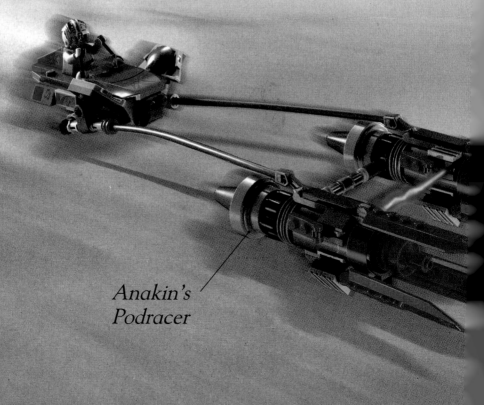

Anakin's Podracer

If Anakin wins the race, his prize
will be freedom from slavery.
He will also win all of the parts
Qui-Gon needs to fix their ship.
Good luck, Anakin!

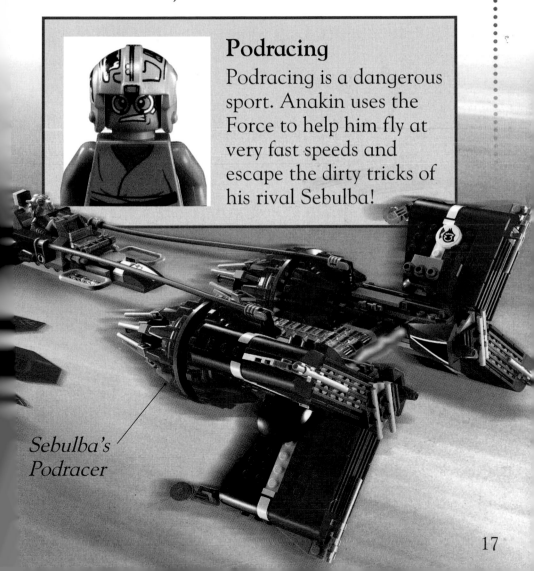

Podracing

Podracing is a dangerous
sport. Anakin uses the
Force to help him fly at
very fast speeds and
escape the dirty tricks of
his rival Sebulba!

*Sebulba's
Podracer*

Mystery man

Hooray! Anakin won the Podrace!
Anakin is free and Qui-Gon has
the parts he needs to fix their ship.
Qui-Gon asks Anakin to come to
the planet Coruscant with him.
He wants Anakin to train as a Jedi.
Hang on, who is this dark figure?
It is Darth Maul! He is a Sith.

Sith probe
droid

Sith
speeder

Qui-Gon duels with Darth Maul. The Sith tests Qui-Gon's lightsaber skills, but he can't defeat the Jedi. Not this time!

Sith Infiltrator

Darth Maul is Darth Sidious's apprentice. His Master orders him to follow the Jedi. He tracks them on his Sith Infiltrator starship.

The Jedi High Council

This is the Jedi High Council. Qui-Gon brings Anakin to Coruscant to meet the Council. Qui-Gon asks the Council to train Anakin as a Jedi because he could be the Chosen One. The Council tests Anakin…

Eeth Koth   Ki-Adi-Mundi   Yoda

Yoda

Yoda is a Jedi Master. He is the oldest and wisest member of the Council. He is more than 800 years old!

…but it does not think Anakin should become a Jedi.
The Council senses that Anakin is too fearful to be a Jedi.

Mace Windu   Saesee Tiin   Plo Koon

Battlefield

It's time to head back to Naboo!
The Gungans of Naboo have
joined the fight for their planet.
The Trade Federation's droid
army battles Gungan soldiers
on the grassy plains of Naboo.

Jar Jar Binks is now a
general of the
Gungan army.
He battles droids
with powerful
energy balls.

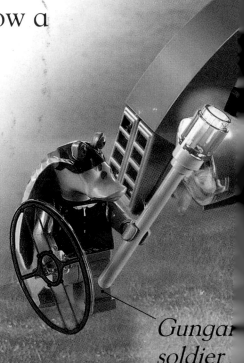

*Gungan
soldier*

It looks like the Gungan army is outnumbered! How will they stop the droid army?

energy
ball

battle
droid

Jar Jar Binks

The Queen's palace

Queen Amidala returns to Naboo. She storms the Royal Palace with the Jedi and Naboo's Head of Security, Captain Panaka.
Can you see Anakin? He is hiding away from the fighting.

Naboo
fighter pilot

Obi-W
Kenobi

Queen
Amidala

Captain
Panaka

Lots of Naboo fighter pilots have been captured by the droid army. Queen Amidala frees them to fight for their planet.

Look out, droids! You are no match for Queen Amidala and her companions.

Qui-Gon Jinn

battle droid

Deadly duel

Look who has appeared at the Royal Palace! It is Darth Maul. He appears to have unfinished business with the Jedi.

The Jedi are highly skilled in lightsaber combat, but so is Maul. He can even fight two Jedi at once with his double-bladed lightsaber!

Qui-Gon is defeated by Maul...

...but Obi-Wan beats Maul in
a fierce duel to the death.
Qui-Gon has one dying wish.
He asks Obi-Wan to train
young Anakin as a Jedi.

Flying high

Where is Anakin now?
He was hiding inside this Naboo
starfighter, but now look!
He is flying it away from Naboo.
Anakin flies into the Trade
Federation's starship above Naboo.
The ship controls the droid army.

R2-D2

This is R2-D2. He is an astromech droid who works for Queen Amidala. He helps Anakin to fly the Naboo starfighter.

BOOM! Anakin destroys the starship's reactor core.
The starship blows up and the droid army is deactivated!

reactor core

The Trade Federation is defeated!
Darth Maul is defeated!
It is time to celebrate on Naboo.

But there is one Sith left in the
galaxy. Where is the mysterious
Darth Sidious?

Darth Sidious has lost his apprentice and now he must replace him with a new one.

Who will it be? And when will the Sith appear again to menace the galaxy?

Glossary

droid
A robot that is programmed to give various kinds of help, for good or for evil!

duel
A battle with weapons, fought between two people.

Gungan
An amphibious creature from the planet Naboo.

hologram
A 3-D image of a person who is not there physically.

lightsaber
A swordlike weapon with a blade of pure energy.

Trade Federation
A powerful and greedy organization that controls business in the galaxy.